VOICE OF REASON

poetry *Pt* today

VOICE OF REASON

Edited by Suzy Walton

First published in Great Britain in 2001 by Poetry
Today, an imprint of
Penhaligon Page Ltd, Remus House, Coltsfoot Drive,
Woodston, Peterborough. PE2 9JX

A Catalogue record for this book is available from the
British Library

ISBN 1 86226 613 1

Typesetting and layout, Penhaligon Page Ltd, England.
Printed and bound by Forward Press Ltd, England

Foreword

Voice Of Reason is a compilation of poetry, featuring some of our finest poets. This book gives an insight into the essence of modern living and deals with the reality of life today. We think we have created an anthology with a universal appeal.

There are many technical aspects to the writing of poetry and *Voice Of Reason* contains free verse and examples of more structured work from a wealth of talented poets.

Poetry is a coat of many colours. Today's poets write in a limitless array of styles: traditional rhyming poetry is as alive and kicking today as modern free verse. Language ranges from easily accessible to intricate and elusive.

Poems have a lot to offer in our fast-paced 'instant' world. Reading poems gives us an opportunity to sit back and explore ourselves and the world around us.

Contents

To Hunt And Not Kill

I used to like hunting, shooting and killing, but now I do not think
it is so hot.

I think about the creatures that over time I have hunted down
and shot.

It seemed good then but it does not anymore, as I think about their
lifeless bodies lying on the floor.

So to all you so called hunters only shoot what you need,
I do not condemn hunting but only shoot what you need to feed.

I have been out with so called hunters who shoot just for fun,
who leave creatures dead and dying on the floor then go
and look for more.

This shooting creatures to extinction so one day these beautiful
creatures will not be there for us to see anymore.

So if you like hunting and shooting, stop, think, about what it is you
do, and how you would feel, if they were hunting you.

So if you still wish to shoot them do with a camera not a gun,
then when you are looking through your photo album,
you will get far more pleasure and more fun.

So to all you so called hunters, look before you leap it could require
far more skill to get a good photo, a treasure you could always keep.

R B Astbury

Welcome To This Country

He was just a boy.
He was young and carefree.
He was walking home happy.
Security cameras caught him skipping
as he made his way through town.
He was a small boy of ten.
He was innocent, trusting.

Somewhere on that journey home
he was attacked.
He was just a child,
but he was stabbed.
A major artery in his leg
was severed with a knife.
People ran away
rather than come to his aid.
They were scared of the blood.

A small boy was left
to crawl on his hands and knees
until he could crawl no more.
A small boy was left
to bleed to death
in a shop doorway alone.

When help finally came,
it was too late to save him.
He'd lost too much blood.
He was dead
before the ambulance arrived
and could take him to hospital.
It's a crying shame,
a sad reflection on our society,
but it was allowed to happen.

He was only a boy,
but he was abandoned to die.
He'd just arrived in England
with his family.
It was his first time out by himself.
Welcome to this country.

Andy Botterill

Default

England, how long before you die
Will our people in the future ask why
How did this come about
No real protest, hardly a shout
A region of Europe beckons now.

Politicians and bureaucrats abound
With few real workers around
Freedoms lost to lies and deceit
England of no fish and little meat
An inheritance just given away.

Politicians and bureaucrats abound
Can jobs for all of them be found
In an England of regions controlled from afar
Will Westminster survive the ensuing cull
Or become an outpost of the dull.

The 'Magna Carta' of King John
Its laws lost and long since gone
Replaced by dictates from our controllers afar
Did the people of England really consent
To its demise, was it meant.

Richard Phillips

The Cause Of This

The genetical scientist experiments.
To get rid of our genes.
Heredity.
With illnesses that are seen.
To weaken our souls.
Freakish, eccentric.
Creations.
Offspring.
Discrimination.
Insight.
Judgement.
Using his gloved hands.
To change the land.
The future of generations to come.
The natural birth choice of parents gone.
Characteristics of our forefathers
turned to dust.
With sensitive and talented
personalities combine.
Banished from a test tube to create.
A frankenstein super-race.

Pat Jones

Untitled

Do we share what we have
with those who have less?
Or do we re-think our generosity
in case we second guess
ourselves through charity and
find ourselves regretting our
open handedness? When we do,
do we feel the power
of guilt that we caress and
then rationalise into nothing?
Reason gives us insight into
reason but there is something
more than reason here: the
call of need to need
we recognise, the sustenance
on which our hearts feed.

Jack Clancy

Try A Smile

Have you noticed when in public places
So many people with expressionless faces
They appear in a world where no others they see
Maybe they have worries, could well be

So many straight faces pass you by
With rarely a smile or twinkle of the eye
Have they forgotten how a kind gesture to make
Like 'Good Morning' the spell of silence to break

When entering a building you hold back the door
Others it won't knock, but you they ignore
They blindly rush by, no handle they touch
With never a thought of 'thanks very much'

The sullen faced staff who work in the store
Consider the customer just a terrible bore
Never a smile or hardly a word do they say
They remain like that till the end of the day

It costs nothing to smile or care a bit
For people who are downhearted, sad and not very fit
To see someone's smiling face, brings in some cheer
It also helps drive away the feeling of loneliness and fear

Perhaps you think your own troubles are great
But there are many worse off in a terrible state
Homeless, ill, dying or poor beyond compare
So smile, cheer up, and of others be aware

Be tolerant and pleasant in every possible way
Show a little thoughtfulness and make someone's day
Give it a try and spread a happy feeling
Remember a broad grin or smile is so very appealing

John Nelson

Protection

Protect us justly from unjust invasion of our person.
But don't make laws that aim to save us from our fears,
Allowing us avoid confronting our own abusers ~
Authority figures, religious guilt and shame,
Our parents, and our peers,
And ourselves, the judge inside our minds
That judges us against perfection.
It's easier to turn our hate on others
Than stop the hating of ourselves;
Since this is when we stop the fight
Against the pain we hate to feel,
And differences in others make them
Attractive targets for unjust persecution.

Robin Graham

Saint George's Day

I don't care if other countries try and bring us down
'The sick man of Europe' with rundown dirty towns
They write about our hooligans, foot and mouth and BSE
Poor railways, bad services, a stuffy monarchy
It doesn't matter anyway, for they cannot take away
Our heritage, our humour, good manners and fair play
They may never see our leafy lanes, or an English village's charm
They just want to paint a picture that will do our image harm
So ignore the jibes for England will always be for me
The country pub, the village fete, ne'er too far from the sea,
Sunday football, test matches, Wimbledon in June
Gardens filled with flowers, tea and scones at noon
Our contribution to music and science and industry
We've so much to be proud of, in our much maligned country.

Marie Knowles

A Reasonable Request

Here but for the grace of God you stand,
Secure in the house of the law,
Sunlit, warm, majestic and divided.
Those cosseted and protected by the state
And we who will obey.
Can this be the house of reason.

And so, in the dark early chill I knelt,
Persuaded by threat, endorsed by force,
Shamed by the wetness beneath my knees,
If I could, I would kill.
This is how reason should be judged,
On knees, in the cold dark and very wet.
A plague on protected politicians,
That is a reasonable request.

Doug Smith

A Poem Towards Peace

A poem towards peace in our land and repartition to God
As I sit in the warmth of the fire light glow
I think of things of this earth I know
Oh! What a state this world is in
Lots of good and much more sin
What will it take to put the world right
It will only come on God's new light
God's own church on earth was split
By a King Henry for his gain no wit
Created a false religion to follow
Never thinking of tomorrow
For four hundred years or more
The state in Ireland is I can but abhor
Protestants pushing Catholic population lower
The majority over minority, just to show their power
So low some resort to ungodly bombing
Not thinking of innocent people coming
Within range of the deadly weapons
Innocently not knowing what is about to happen
Men, Women, Children even animals killed
Being blown to bits hospitals being filled
People like Paisley their pulpits on Sundays
Telling his people to take gun ways
The Catholic church does not preach war
The Holy Fathers messages of peace from shore to shore
Peace in the World can come only one way some day
Our Lord Jesus Christ came to show the way
He spoke 'No man can go to My Father except by me'
The true Church of God, this church has to be
Looking into the scriptures and into history
Before and after he founded his church, you can find this a mystery
This was only possible because he was the Son of God, you will find
As Henry has left his followers in the lurch
With no redemption power in his self styled church
Nor did he die for mankind on a wooden cross

R T Owen

11

Shadowed Corners Of Fear

I think of those in shadowed corners,
Hiding from the fearful nights, here and there.
Afraid to face the neon city ~ day by day,
Imaged now with coloured lights, around us.

It's always the same questions, the longing for an answer.
The intricacy of the labyrinth to find my own Truth is almost
                                                    too much.
The path is not dark, merely jaded as all routes blend to one, my
                                                destiny regular.
I can hear it, it's so repressed, as if being smothered, or drowned.
A voice that soothes me, lulls my fear.

Humanity is ever searching for peace.
With the constant threat of wars and famine.
The whole world is now constantly threatened by upheavals,
                                                also homeless.
Our every wakening hour is full of turmoil and fear.
With no hope in our hearts ever, there can be no peace in our minds.

We're constantly clambering for something bigger and better in
                                                    our lives.
No one however powerful can escape the constant threats to
                                                their lives.

I think of those who're in cardboard boxes ~
Vagrant wrapped in paper sheets, and rags.
Escaping from the neon city ~ cold and damp.
To sanctuary of cobbled streets.

I've an ache, in my body, my mind, even my soul cannot escape.
I feel it deep, I know what it is.
Why can't they admit it, just for a moment?
The pain has become quiet; I try to suppress the want inside me.
It seems so simple, it is a word.
Help! Help me, help me now, also help others too?

We live in an era of high technology ~
More leisure time, less money to spend.
Alas there is much sadness in the lives of mankind.

As we approach the life of hardship, with no sign of peace in
                                                            our hearts.
Where do we go from here you might ask.
But no one seems to be listening to our pleas.

It's time the governments of our world, listened to its people's pleas,
                                                            why not?
You're paid by us, why don't you help the people out, not your
                                                            own pockets.

I think of those still lost and lonely.
Searching for their bread daily, not like you're.
Drifters from neon city need your help now!
Who from modern life have fled, only the poor.

The days seem longer, but the nights scare us.
I've held in my tender, emotional thoughts now for so long,
                                                how would you do?
When I'm alone with only my thoughts, what're you doing?
I don't know how to express warmth, or to eat so well.
I keep pondering the past, where am I going.
What should you've done?
What could you've done?
Speak the truth now!
Do something now!
It seems so simple, put your hearts to the test.

It's time wars and rumour or wars was driven from our lands,
                                                homeless also in our lives.
Our world is dark and dreary, cold and hard,
There is hope in our people's hearts, do you feel the same.
In the final analysis peace will only come if mankind makes a kind
conscious effort to combat hate, fear, and wars, by hardship and
homeless, from our lives.

I think of those who've done no wrong ~
Yet suffer pain and woe.
Escaping from the neon lights ~ into a home.
But where is there to go, for everyone?

With *love* in your hearts, *Peace* in your minds,
Faith in our future, and *Charity* for the less fortunate ones!
Will anybody try to help?
Is the world really in such a state?

Should go forward, and not backward, to greet the new year with ~
                                        Renewed Hope!
Shadowed Corners Be No More In The World!

   V Borer

Zaire

Speak to me and reassure us all,
That you're gonna make it right,
Broadcast on all forms
That you've found the key to their plight.

Go on, it's a must ~ inform the nation
That everything'll be okay.
Succour the banks and industries and richies,
That they might vote for you one day.

Help me understand the inability to act,
That what you haven't done is good.

Articulate the 'whens' and whys'
And 'hows' and 'whats'
That are gonna change the world.

Indulge me, tease me, please me.
As if that'll make me feel just a little bit better.

And if you still haven't found the answer
After all that trying,
Then tell me what you say to the mother
Of a child, whose gravestone reads:

'Born yesterday,
Dead today.'

  S Moralee

You Know Who You Are!

My stomach churns, I feel sick inside, as the time approaches eight.
Soon I'll have to make that walk, past *them* at the school gate.
They will be there, calling names and shoving me around.
I wish *they* would leave me alone and find someone else to hound.

I don't know why *they* picked on me, or what I'm supposed to
have done.
They make me cry, *they* steal my things and think it's all great fun.
My confidence has ebbed away, I can't concentrate in school.
It's getting worse, there's no escape, *they* think it makes them cool.

I used to have lots of friends, but now they are too scared to speak.
They hurry past and avert their eyes, like I am some kind of freak.
I realise they are worried and afraid to show concern.
If they are seen to talk to me, it soon might be their turn!

I make it home, the phone rings, Mum says there is no one there!
But I know, if I pick it up, *they* will threaten me and swear.
When I am in the house alone, *they* keep coming to the door.
They ring and knock and shout at me, I can't stand it any more!

I have to get away from *them*, this torment has to cease.
Do I have to end it all, to find come kind of peace?
They will not stop, *they* do not care, *they* let it go too far.
They are bullies and *they* are cowards and *they* know who *they* are!

Yvonne Granger

Victims

The spirit of Gandhi survived India,
The spirit of Kennedy survived Dallas,
Yet we still do not know why men bear malice,
So let's drink of truth's golden chalice,
While poor men live in slums,
And a rich man lives in a palace,
Yet still the truth comes,
Yet we're still looking for the holy grail,
A time to end wars ~ to no avail,
Whilst tramps loiter at the bar,
And you're crushed to death in a streetcar,
I dream of an end to atomic war,
Two old soldiers engaged in a brawl,
They up and heeded their country's call,
Now reduced to raking bins,
I hear the scrape of violins,
For these two old has-beens,
They've thrown away their medals,
Now whilst in drugs he peddles,
A life in ruins,
The sun doth swelter,
But nowhere do they find shelter,
Fighting over food scraps,
I look askance at these two chaps,
War claims many victims,
But surely you're better to be dead,
Than on the street begging for bread.

Alan Pow

I Will Be Free

I will say what I want to say
    That is my right,
I will protest against injustice
    And put up a fight.

I will make myself heard
    If I possibly can,
We must all speak out
    Against injustice to man.

Nothing will silence me,
    That is my right,
Intimidation won't work,
    Nor will fright.

Free speech is our heritage,
    The essence of life,
To speak against repression
    Keeps us from strife.

Dianne Core

Ode To The Planet

This magical beautiful planet,
  Spinning in majesty,
Sings glory to its maker
  If we would let it be.
Stop torturing its forests,
  Ruining its seas.
Polluting all its rivers
  Its leafy glens and leas.
Give earth chance to recover
  From man's inherent greed,
Let beauty reign triumphant
  O'er every hill and mead.

Maureen Oglesby

OK Jack

I'm strong and fit, that's easy to see
And other mens' failings don't bother me.
You have physical problems? Well ~ what a shame.
It's sad, it's bad but I'm not to blame.
You'll just have to manage; I'll look away
To hell with you Jack ~ I'm OK.

I am a bigot ~ it's all in the game
When I mock your creed or call you a name.
I am esteemed among my peers
And never the butt of their jibes and sneers.
If I see you in trouble I look away.
Fend for yourself Jack, I'm OK.

I am solvent. I'm comfortably set
And other folks' problems I soon forget.
Why should I worry when poor men cry
With hunger and cold. Well, they should try
To keep out of sight and out of my way.
To hell with your tears Jack ~ I'm OK.

This is my conscience ~ I hear it say
'You will reap what you sow another day.
The victims; the helpless; the suffering tide
Reach out to your heart and won't be denied.
Do what you must; don't walk away ~
Then they like you Jack, might be OK.'

V Finlay

Numbers Versus Names

When I was born my dad gave me his name.
I got my own as well, so that made two.
When I married my third name to me came.
And those three seemed to me as if they'd do.

Yet now not names but numbers are the thing,
And the Powers That Be excuses just won't buy.
So if aught to their notice we would bring,
Their digits we must use to catch their eye.

The Club Book and the Health Unit feature on the list,
National Insurance, Library, Council Tax,
PIN, the Union, the Bank, the DSS,
The Post Code and the Telephone, and if we have a Fax.

This list could be endless, and maybe even will,
If we let ourselves become ciphers in the great Computer Mill.

Fae D Watson

Decisions Time Again
(Sequel to Decisions Decisions 1997)

I want to do what is for the best
Again I am being put to the test
I'll have to turn on the radio
To hear this time the way to go?

Does anyone know what to do?
They keep on saying 'It's down to you'
The responsibility on my shoulders
Is weighing me down like ten ton boulders!

I'm feeling quite blue about turning red
Then perhaps it's more sensible what the orange one said?
They all say they are right and the other one's wrong
Then all sing with gusto the party song.

Blue says vote for him, he is your man
We won't keep the Euro but then perhaps we can
Then red comes along in a double decker bus
Shouting much louder and waving at us.

Lots of new policies to digest
The one who is talking is always the best
Should we carry on or stay as we are
Or would making a change be going too far?

Perhaps orange will solve it he's a sensible chap
He is level headed and not prone to scrap
Trying to choose is making me dizzy
My hair is standing on end like frizzy Lizzy.

June 7th is approaching ~ there's a local one too
Means thinking twice which is difficult to do
I will try to be calm ~ not get the colours in a mix
And put the right party with the right kiss X!

Barbara Fosh

Fashion Of Today

As I stand here and look around, no cheerfulness do I see.
The drab and dreary clothes they wear,
All black and dark you have to stare, really most forlornly.
Where have all the colours and brightness in our clothes gone.
There was a time when lovely colours brightly shone.
No more I am so sad to say.
No one thinks it is good to look bright and gay.
These awful deadly colours of black and grey.
It makes you think of funerals and clothes in disarray.
So come on You Folk, and lighten up.
Put the colours back into our Gear.
Then I will not need to stand just here,
To watch the fashions pass in fear.

Zoe French

Help

How long before the end of the world,
Nothing is ever put back,
Everything is always taken
All down to money (I think)
How long before we all realise this big company's,
Massive destruction,
All killing the Planet
All down to greed (I think)
How long before we all realise this
Not too long (I hope)

Paul Morris

What Is It . . .
(For Julie Harrison, a dear friend)

To follow in your phosphorous wake
Life . . . is the risk we take
For our existence
. . . We earn a pittance . . .
. . .Receive little . . .
Is this our reward
Is this . . . how it shall be
Welcome to the real World

To take your hand
We'll take each other
In a flurry of white . . .
To say . . . 'I love you . . .'
Publicly declare and mean it . . .
The only reason for existence . . .
In a world . . . That isn't sure if it really exists at all
Was you . . .

Welcome to limbo
We have our problems here
Though in the shadows . . .
I'll hold you near for you are dear . . .
Doomed forever . . . running a race it cannot ultimately win
The human race . . . in suspended animation
Is this life . . . no it's the real world
Unlock your silence
  This is our existence . . .

  Sally Wyatt

Nonconformist

The one who stands out from the rest,
The one most think is odd.
The one who many detest
And say he thinks he's God!
The one who never will conform
And in thought is not myopic.
The one who isn't of the norm
And becomes some people's topic.
The one whose views will be ignored
As most live for the day,
And find such views make them bored
And insist he goes away.

This country has throughout the years
Had such nonconformists,
One was ignored which led to tears
Due for foreign extremists.
A lunatic for all to see
Created military might,
And we were warned what would be
Which turned out to be right.

Now of course it won't be war
For that country to rule,
It's finance that will make us poor
Which they'll be given by the fool.
The nonconformist still will warn
But proboscis alas are short.
A new era will be born
But will we learn or be distraught!

D R Thomas

Hello To Earth

As I look across the fields and hills
I wonder how much man really kills
He rapes and plunders the countryside
Builds roads and bridges far and wide

Do we want to look at fields of green
Or cars and lorries? I want to scream!
Leave the meadows and valleys alone
For so many animals this is their home

Where will they go when there's no pastures left
And the land is ravaged and bereft?
The badger, the stoat, the rabbit, the hare
For these and more we have to care

They can't protest and have a rally
Hold up banners saying 'Save our Valley'
They can't hold sit-ins or argue their case
They need help from us ~ the human race

But man cuts down the forests and pollutes the oceans
There are still some of us though who have notions
Of a world where there's room for the grass to grow
The flora to flourish, the rivers to flow

So let's join together and make a stand
To nurture and cherish our precious land
Our valleys and hills and seas and streams
Must not only appear in our dreams

Our children must see more than steel and tarmac
For them, for the animals let's get our land back
If only the roads could be turned back to turf
Goodbye to pollution, hello to earth.

Ann Thornton

Disappearance

Where have they all gone to ~ does anybody know
Once there was lots of them standing row by row.
Once there was lots of them built for people who are ill,
Or simply just too old and weak to climb the wooden hill.
Now when people buy them what's the first thing that they do
Put in dormer windows and an en suite shower with loo.
No one wants to build them because the profit is not there
Very soon they will all be gone the house without a stair.
How do we stop extinction does anybody know
Let's rally round and save it the British bungalow.

Les Orme

On My Soap Box

Yes I would speak of salvation
Tell others how Jesus died for all,
And by His blood ~ you can be set free
You young, you old, you weak, you poor.

I'd tell you to get ready
And take Jesus into your heart,
For some day soon He will come again
Sinner turn to Jesus
In your life let Him take part.

I'll talk out loud and clear
For Jesus said 'I am the way
The truth and life'
'So come sinners find Jesus Christ.'

Do not rot in a black hell of smoke
Open your heart's door right now
~ I'd say ~
Do come unto Jesus don't rot away.

Call unto the Lord right now
He is your only hope,
He will put your life
The right way round
And help you how to cope.

Marion Staddon

Ode To Politicians

Tories, the amateur professional,
Labour, the Professional amateur,
Lib-Dems, amateur amateurs, and banal,
all mostly dishonest, talking manure,
why pay them? They represent the few,
whatever political view, it's the same,
never averse to telling a lie or two,
MP cannot sit, without the tabloid pain,
lies and smears fired at each other,
this, the right dishonourable member,
why? It makes you endlessly wonder,
unreliable from January to December,
overpaid on whatever side they sit,
politicians do not earn our respect,
why have other jobs, supplementing it?
With MPs like this, what do you expect,
one historical figure made a blunder,
these people with the verbal diarrhoea,
sometimes it makes you really wonder,
that Guy Fawkes had the right idea!

Christopher Higgins

Student Life
(Dedicated to all my friends at Derby)

Bored, dull, unsociable being are we,
No, quite the opposite, you will soon see.
At the bar, pubs or night-clubs every night,
Having a laugh, lads looking for a fight.
Noisy, loud, we live through it all, every day,
Working for our beer money, with our pay.
Grants, fees, we fight to have privileges to study for a degree,
But the government are nasty, cruel and very greedy.
Getting our money to reach a budget, increasing their pay
We demonstrate for our rights, but no-one listens to our say.
Studying life in which we live in, gives us an overview,
To what is in store for us, and what the future is too.
But after the lessons, we forget the woes and the worries,
And drink lots of beers and then go for some curries.

Suzanne Shepherd

Street Moles: 1997

This year it seems is Roadworks Year!
And periodically whole hordes of men are here.
In January 1997 we had BT,
It appears they drink a lot of tea.
In March the Gasmen did lots of digging,
Pipes were everywhere, as was their rigging.
May had arrived, a Water Board invasion,
If you wanted a reason they're good at liaison.
Then we tolerated Eurobell,
And whatever they did we never can tell!
When all this lot went there was peace in our ward,
But then our hackles rose up, the Electricity Board.
They'd just arrived to dig some trenches,
And sat quite frequently on makeshift benches.
It's December now, all gangs gone at last,
And to the whole of them I wish, Happy Christmas!

N T Membury

Great Britain?

What has happened to this wonderful isle?
The island we were proud to call Great,
Even give up our lives for.
It has become a cement block,
Over-crowded with population explosion,
A blot on the horizon.
Stony-broke, where pensioners and homeless abound,
Others build Mansions, etc at our expense.
The rich get richer, the poor get poorer.
The EU drags us further down,
While Brussels Bosses have their rules
Which poor old Britain must observe.
Give us a Government which will obey
The people who voted them in,
Give us the Health service, get Rid of Crime,
Let us have our Pride and our Greatness back,
God save the Queen, let's salute our Flag.

Meriel J Brown

Foot And Mouth

One Hundred days have now gone by,
Since Foot and Mouth caused stock to die;
But did some know that all not well,
Yet still sent stock from towns to fells?

The neighbourhood culls have caused some tears,
To rebuild stock will take some years;
What really causes disease to spread,
Do germs live on when animals dead?

Those TV pictures filled our screens,
Of slaughtered animals, going all green;
For many days those carcasses lay,
Pictures of ruin, of sadness, dismay.

Toxic fumes from burning pyres,
Brought an end to burning fires;
Large deep craters on chosen sites,
Army brought in to help the fight.

The lies and deception all scattered around,
Chaos and heartbreak throughout has been found;
Enquiries, if thorough, when disease truly clear,
May show loss of thousands, but will someone hear?

Stories of barbaric methods, used to kill some stock,
Caused some real revulsion, brought on many shocks;
We will not know the outcome, of horrors brought to light,
Till election days are over, we discover the true right.

Do we learn the lessons, so clear from before,
In nineteen sixty seven and during the last war;
My memories so vivid, as Foot and Mouth found,
Within forty-eight hours, all buried in the ground.

John Paulley

Justice Today

Self defence is no offence
Is what the victims say
But the Lord Justice said that you hit back
And for that my dear you'll have to pay

You were only doing what you thought right
Protecting your life in the dead of the night
But the Lord Justice said you dealt the blow
That hurt that little mugger so

You were protecting your children to the core
When the paedophile moved in next door
But the Lord Justice said you threw that paint
And made him out to be a saint

You were only doing what you thought fit
When you gave that burglar a little kick
But the Lord Justice said you ruptured his spleen
And that from a little kick had never been seen

You were only protecting your life
When you turned on him his kitchen knife
But the Lord Justice said you mutilated his face
Knocked him about and sprayed him with mace

So as you sit in the dock and wait
While over your future they deliberate
Remember of this sorry tale
Remember it's the victim British Justice will *fail*

Gillian Morphy

freedom of speech

it's the one thing we've got
it's the one thing to use
to air our views
to try and reach out
to encourage debate
let's not leave things
safe in the closet
let's get them out
dust them off and be brave
let them hear us *scream*
let them hear us *shout*
it's worth fighting for

from the words of this poem
to the words of a song
don't let the powers that be
tell us what's right and wrong

it's the one thing we've got
it's the one thing to use
to air our views
to encourage debate
don't leave things unsaid
it might cause some to squirm
but if you really believe
love can conquer hate
so onwards and forwards
let them hear us *sing*
let them *see* our words
after all, it's worth fighting for

we've not got much
so don't let them take it away

   p j gassner

Britain Shall Stand

God gave to us this pleasant land
Of moors, hills, rivers, sea and strand,
Proudly see our flag unfurled
Symbol of strength in a hostile world.

Bravely stand we against the foe
As we did before, long years ago ~
Battered, bleeding, still we stood
In mutual faith and brotherhood.

In the meadows, down the lane
Scattered amid the swelling grain
See the poppies, glowing red ~
Tributes to those whose blood was shed.

Happily they lived, gallantly died,
Phalanxes of brothers side by side,
Nothing had they but their lives to give ~
Everything ~ all ~ that we might live.

Will their sacrifice have been in vain?
Do we have to embark on war again?
Yes, if God is at our side
In the struggle for freedom and Britain's pride.

No enemy yoke will we humbly bear,
Nor foe shall sully this land we hold dear,
A small folk, we, who inherited this land
But by God's grace, Britain shall stand.

Pauline Brown

The Poverty Trap

I see a band of pale-faced
And weary men all dwindled down
By days increasing in their weight.
No sustenance, no dwelling place
For generosity is rare.
I watch them brooding over death
Or living still on charity.
I'm waiting for their hearts to break
As, sick in soul and body both,
They pray for immortality
Because my name is Poverty.

I kneel beside an ancient crone
Who stays alive through strength of will.
She mumbles 'twixt her toothless gums
Until two icy lips are still.
As vultures glide above their prey,
I swoop on unprotected men
Who sink into oblivion
Or cease to care until they die.
They know that all their lives will be
For ever in my cunning trap
Because my name is Poverty.

Her spotless steps are scrubbed each day.
Imperfect clothes are darned and patched.
She manages to find a way
To pay her bills. I take a look
Into her eyes and see the pride
Still gleaming there, refusing help.
I know I cannot break her will,
As children scamper in the dirt
Or laugh with untold happiness
Until they learn subservience,
Because my name is Poverty.

Nancy Reeves

Untitled

Lovest Thou me? Then feed my flock,
Not earthly food, would I have thee know,
The Bread of Life, them freely give,
As I gave them Myself, long years ago,
The Bread of Love, take ye, and eat,
Never more hungry, shall ye be,
Seekest thou far, and feed My sheep,
If thou wouldst My disciple be.

L Page

Into The Future

Mummy what's a primrose?
It used to be a pretty flower, that grew down banks of streams.
But now it's just in picture books, and older people's dreams.

Daddy what's a sky lark?
In days gone by a tiny bird, but at singing one of the best.
Since the countryside has been destroyed, no place to build its nest.

Excuse me Mr Scientist.
What happened to the dragonflies and the busy bumblebees.
Why did you allow acid rain to poison all the trees?

Hey! Mr Richman.
Why are we living in this plastic dome, why did no one really care?
It seems a simple basic need, to breathe in pure clean air.

Order! Order! To all MPs.
You have denied me all these pleasures, lost forever I suppose.
I'll never see a spider's web, or smell a rose.

God's Plan B23/7.
The ants and the mosquitoes are cool and lying low.
More sensible of earth's creatures, just wait for *man* to *go!*

Gordon Nixon

Time Waster

Whoever conjured up
The *census?*
Potty questions all
Quite senseless.
A hundred years
Before it's clear.
I can't care less
I won't be here.

Corinne Lovell

Cant

A 'cull', they call it
Not 'kill', not 'slaughter',
Not the wanton, wasteful shedding of precious life blood on
                                                    the ground,
But a cull, just . . . a cull.

Oh, the *cant* contained in cull!
The bamboozle, the cheating,
The *trickery* of it ~
Debasing our language to manipulate our minds!

The meaning of 'cull' is to select and gather ~
As when one picks sweet flowers for a scented bouquet.
The opposite of 'cull' is to reject ~ repudiate ~ throw away ~ and
That is what is being done, this blood-spilling spring.

They relentlessly reject ewes with their lambs,
They cast away cows with their calves,
They sentence the sows, with their litters, to *become* litter ~
The very opposite of culling!

A million creatures have climbed the ramp, in the space of a
                                                    hundred days,
Like the millions who walked the ramp in the holocaust.
Such slaughter was the 'final solution', for which they reaped
                                                    economic gain
By culling the gold teeth, the hair, the jewellery . . .

So too, these trusting animal souls,
Dependent on their owners to keep them alive,
Are being repudiated on a parallel, putrid, pyre
To pursue pounds and pence!

It is a crooked cant ~
To put a sugary slant on killing
By calling it *culling!*
Such stock phrases are the dialogue of thieves.

This jangling, dissonant, cant
Is a sad song ~ a *dirge* ~ for the beasts
But, more than that, it has become
A grotesque parody of humanity.

    Bettine Symons

A Vampyric Dilemma

Everyone dying, no fresh blood to be had
The plague's taken hold and all good blood gone bad
Corpses diseased lay strewn all about
How can I thrive in this pestilent drought?

A Vampyric dilemma, cannot drink from deceased
But all still alive are unpure and diseased.
I grow weaker and weaker as the plague grows still worse,
But although times are hard I shall live through this curse,
I was bestowed a great gift when my master drunk me,
I possess the power of immortality!

I shall flee this decaying city and return upon my home,
To the Carpathian mountains where mine ancestors did roam,
I shall settle there a while till this epidemic dies,
Then return again to the place where my heart lies . . .

And there I'll feed on new-born blood
The purest of the pure,
And on the misty streets of Londinium . . .
My name shall be whispered once more!

*Star**

Freedom Of Speech

Who does this country belong to?
'Raise the flag' our men cried,
For this so many died
Shops used to have a wide open door,
Too many charity shops are now a bore,
Rubbish in the street
Could hurt a pensioner's feet.
If everyone tried very hard
'Come to Britain' would be on the card,
'Vote for me' is now the cry
Next day they have forgotten us. Why?
No men in Parliament for a year,
All women! What have they to fear!?
Families should come first
Not 'I'm off to the pub *I've got a thirst.'*
Think of your children
Someday there will be great-grandchildren
Would they enjoy rubbish like ours?
Or play in the parks for many happy hours.
Someone who is honest we need,
Who will give us a real lead
Maybe, just maybe!
It will happen one day to you and me!

Margaret Pearce

Our Shame
(Dedicated to Damilola Taylor)

In a well in a staircase
the little boy lay
With a sliced artery in his leg
his life ebbed away.

Concrete for company
is all that he had
As he lay all alone
and slowly bled.

Outrage is what we all feel
for the perpetrators of this crime
For the death of this child
who died in the grime.

A fifty-thousand pound bounty
they've placed on their heads
The hunt's on for the weapon
and any clues where they're led.

For just three months
he had lived on this estate
On a deprived, crime-ridden area
where he met his fate.

He was jeered, he was bullied
from the time that he came
Was the colour of his skin
the crime that they blame?

His parents bereft, inconsolable
    forlorn
Weep in despair
their youngest has gone.

A shy boy, they say
both loving and quiet
Died all alone
right out of sight.

Now he's at peace with the
good Lord above
We know he won't suffer
as never he should.

Shame on our country that
this happened here
Let's unite in our efforts
so children can live without fear.

Gloria Hargreaves

Freedom Of Speech

How satisfying to find this dry-skinned frame
with all its awkward aches and pernickety pains
can survive four years and blossom again.
How sweet to know these stiffening limbs
which increasingly creak with conspicuous clarity
can still evoke such avid attention and
stimulate an avalanche of overdue charity

Rejoice my re-admission to the human race
celebrate my re-appearance with Sanatogen wine
fete me with promises and adaptable agendas
feign felicitous perturbation and marry me to your manifesto,

Cover me with placards, pin me with badges
wash me in verbiage, swill me in soundbites,
cajole me, coax me, blandish and beguile me,
entice me, seduce me, flatter and tempt me
collect me, drive me, deliver me to the booth
push me to the table and the lady with the list
humour me and honour me and return me to retirement.
Stick me in the corner in my Shackleton chair
bring me my slippers and a strong cup of tea
and ignore or endure my persistent protesting
the whining and the moaning of this irrational voice
and thank God for my irrelevance till next polling day:

Tom Eadie

Smelly Smoke

Burning Pyres of loving creatures
Is so unkind to all,
No one knows the stress involved
Unless you are one.

Baby Lambs and Baby Calves
Born into this world,
Were shot and then burnt
Through no fault of their own.

People that are not involved
Don't understand the stress,
That farmers go through this
Because of Politics.

Some unresponsible person
Has ruined many lives,
They have not an inkling
Of true Country Life.

The Country is unstable
With lack of Moo and Mee,
That years and years of emptiness
Will never be the same.

Mair Griffiths

Spin Doctors, Spin

I'm on a fact-finding mission
The more I look, the less I see
I'm only given permission
To access virtual reality

Cry baby, cry
Spin doctors, spin
In a world of illusion
Nobody wins . . .

I'm on a fact-finding mission
The more I hear, the less I like
The politicians with 'vision'
It's just another sound bite

Cry baby, cry
Spin doctors, spin
In a world of illusion
Nobody wins . . .

I'm on a fact-finding mission
The more I ask, the less I'm told
The meaning of their decisions
Down the river we've been sold

Cry baby, cry
Spin doctors, spin
In a world of illusion
Nobody wins . . .

Celeste Devereux

Third World Pity

We hear of drought and starvation in the Third World
We are shocked
We click our tongues and shake our heads
Then weep at moving images
Of pot-bellied walking dead
Wide-eyed, skinny and wrinkled
Emaciated by lack of food
Dehydrated from lack of water
And yes, we'll give some money to Oxfam
As soon as we can
We'll clear out our wardrobes
And send our cast-off's to charity shops.

Exonerated by our caring
And deep feelings of humanity
We go about our daily lives
And after dinner
We'll swill away the leftover food
From our overfilled plates
With running water from a tap
And, if it's a nice day water the plants
And wonder what we'll have
For supper.

Carole Wale

Sugar's Platform

My mind exists so the next
time that I hear
no laughter again, due
to the troubles, locked
beneath a man's body.
Gather around the literate.
This sort of art,
destroys rebellion.
Weaving passed silence is
the tragic fool's world.
Sending word alone,
is possible.

Kirk Antony Watson

Talk, Talk

If you hear the schoolkids at playtime,
Happily playing and chattering away,
On subjects wide and diverse,
Years of conversations lie ahead for them,
As they develop and discover our universe,

As they grow and mature,
They discuss and debate,
Every subject under the sun,
From the atom bomb to,
How much faster will man run,

They can pour scorn on,
The government of the day,
Or heap praise, as the case may be,
Or talk about famines or floods,
Or discuss the plight of the family marooned above the
Waters up a tree,

They could offer up a prayer,
Or sing their favourite song,
They could just join in,
And sing with the others, 'we shall not be moved,'
Or debate the life and times of Ho Chi Minh,

The freedom of speech,
Has not always been ours by right,
Men have fought, to give us this chance,
To gossip or chat or converse,
To ask a question, or book our tickets in advance,

They may discuss the weather,
The cost of living,
Decide on which university course to sit,
Find some common ground with an angry neighbour,
Or join a Christmas parade with candles lit.

P J Littlefield

Old Timer's Disease

One day the young ones will have to face
The cruel comments they made about the elders of their race
Cutting criticisms that the old are a waste of space
For one day they too will come to see
That the 'old timer's disease' is disagreeable, even to the elderly
It's a time of swift decline, with a sign marked, 'This Way to Eternity'
For it's no joke when your senses and limbs start to fail
The once able you, is now getting frail
That hale and hearty you cease to be
Your heart may be willing, but your body won't pay the fee
And your mind's lost somewhere out there
As through a time lost window you sit and stare
Remembering that love belongs only to the young and fair
All that the juveniles declare is the smell of urine and decay in the air
So children look carefully, wait and see, that pitiful person might be
you or me

Don't think these poor people elderly and alone,
Would be better off, hidden in a nursing home
Or better still deep underground,
Sleeping with the worms, cold but safe and sound.
Remember that time is ever future bound
For old age forever creeps, to finally offer us eternal sleep
So old timer's, Alzheimer's, call it what you please
Is an anti-social disease, with all its failing faculties
With thoughts trapped in distant memories
Their present condition marked 'Not aware'
Returned to a second childhood, but do we care?
Isn't it a pity, such a dreadful crime
When your mind and body's sell by date,
Is marked 'Too Old ~ *rejected* ~ out of time

John Pegg

The 'Blair Government'

Have you ever experienced a government like this?
It is so politically correct it's difficult to exist.
Don't mention marriage or the traditional family,
It's much more acceptable to be single and gay.

This is the government that believes in everything,
Yet it seems to have convictions about nothing.
Parliament Act to lower the age of consent,
No need to protect your child is the argument.

Fuel prices sky high, enough to cause mass protest,
No one believes Gordon's lie 'It's all in our interest'.
On top of this, the fuel companies don't give a damn,
It's their profits that matter, not the average man.

These days it's cool to have liberal views,
Being conservative doesn't make the news.
We are the new trendy modernists of this age,
Whatever the consequences, we have the stage.

This is the 'Blair government' that controls your mind,
A more arrogant government will be hard to find.
We have no beliefs; we are the kings of spin,
We say all things to all people and you vote us in.

Simon Icke

Oops

Will the Government retch
On the words of its speech
A creature so out of control
Just more of the same
Of the rich man's poor game
Where lie its heart and its soul
The greed of a land
Pours through fingers like sand
Every woman and man come sit sat
Talk in equalities name
When poor all the same
Then hypocrisy comes and all that
Same song is all sung
When on bottom rung
Till temptation of money
Its dream
All forget where they were
As men call them Sir
Democracy and its gradients of schemes
So talk of the sin
Till the pennies roll in
To become an idiot like them
As you climb up a step
Another slips down on the wet
We're all getting giddy again
On and on it all goes
As man on death row
Denies of the rope with a trick
And we're just the same
Play America's game
We blame all the workless and sick
As the fat get more fat
As an overfed cat

They mess in the face of the poor
But never you mind
Charity's kinder than kind
As Blair does the same as before
Can they live with their guilt
Was Jerusalem built
On an England so pleasant and green
We still sing the song
Amid all of the wrong
Who laughs at the thought of a dream
I could go right on
Till this verse was so long
It would take twenty pages of text
Can you get the gist
I'm so thoroughly p****d
One thing I ain't is perplexed

Raymond Peter Walker

Depleted Uranium

This world of ours will never be safe,
We give our soldiers, DU munitions, without faith,
Then not tell them of the risks,
Depleted Uranium was not their wish,
They handle shells, or breathe in the dust,
They will all die, fall ill, all fuss.

Exposure levels were too high,
Our soldiers all, are going to die,
Cancerous, or ill, the MOD don't care,
But could not tell them ~ would not dare,
Must defeat the enemy . . . the foreign foe,
Those soldiers all ~ they had to go.

How many more shells will be made?
With radioactive elements, which is forbade,
Our technicians and scientists will not tell,
All our soldiers, of this living hell,
We need the truth for all today,
This horrendous mistake will not go away.

John Harper-Smith

The Battle Of Britain Continues

In 1940, Britain was a historic inspiration,
But, in 2001, the country calls for explanation.

Europe still seems an annoying threat.
We haven't levelled up with it yet.
The quality of our NHS,
Education and railways is less.
We have more single, teenage mummies;
Football thugs and drug-powered dummies.
When BSE and foot and mouth here abounded,
The continentals were all just left astounded.
For many things, we British pay more
Than they do in a cross-channel store.

For the freedom we hard won them 56 years ago,
Could our neighbours now help liberate us from all this woe?

Allan Bula

Political Correctness

To have 'PC' is trendy
But then, it's something more!
Ah! Yes ~ if you're not careful
You could be 'up-in-court;
Describing wrong ~ a title
Or voicing a retort
That Brussels deems offensive
To someone ~ or some folk
Like weighing fruit in kilos
Not pounds ~ or you'll invoke
A reprimand ~ as I did
When teaching 'drawing-to-scale';
The present 'HMI' observed
My reference thus to fail
To name the 'Blackboard' *chalk*board
(Though black its colour be)
I duly was reported
And censured *'not PC'*.

Frances Cox

Truth From The Darkness

Talking about nothing at all.
Staring into space, beyond reality and reason.
Speaking truth with no oppression,
No logic at all, no lies to hold.
Open truth of a life to live,
Free from rules and regulations.
Open mind, no boundaries or chains.
The world is free for all, who wish to see her,
See the beauty in the flowers and rain.
In the open desert or crowded plane,
Truth within the hearts of men.
Peace where enemies once reigned,
Love where hate once ate the soul.
Tears of laughter instead of pain.
A smile that lights up the darkest day,
Or night with a broken heart.
Where colours brighten the dull of the land,
Just like night time turns into day.
Talking and seeing nothing at all,
Staring beyond reality and reason.
A place where truth has no oppression,
No logic at all; nor lies to hold.
To a world full of bright colours,
With only tears of love and laughter.
Where hatred has no room at all,
But peace covers all the world.

A M Williamson

Why?

Why did I think that I had found
The freedom I deserved,
What made me think, that I achieved
The right to open speech,
Freedom of mind,
Freedom of action.
How do I explain to me this violent reaction.
How come the mask has slipped,
To show a stranger's face.
The voice I hear is not the same
Those eyes are full of hate.
A public house, too many beers
Once more have sealed my fate.
How can I stand another day,
To smile and be polite,
Pretending, that it was not late
And say, all is alright.
Not me, not anymore am I,
The villain who provokes,
With just one word,
It was hello,
And then all hell broke loose.

Jardene

Walk On

Politicians are travelling
Across the land
Singing their praises
To their fellow man
The countryside
Is in mourning
Spring lambs
Are burning
The earth is weeping
Man is not grieving
Power is his command
A nation is making noises
Politicians reign
In high places
Following their devices
Walk on young man
Take your stand
Hold the dream
In your hand.

Yvonne Moore

Freedom Of Speech

The natural world around us responds
People of the globe smile carefreely
Creativity and skills unite
When freedom of speech prevails.

The order of things lives happier
Humanity no longer wrapped in fear
Ideologies no longer stifled
When freedom of speech matters

Margaret Ann Wheatley

Lost Religion

I don't pray for starving Children
Whose bones stick through their flesh
Who quietly lay with sorrowful eyes
And wait for lingering death
I don't pray for land-slide victims
Buried beneath tons of mud
I don't pray for relatives who search
For survivors of a flood
I don't pray to end ethnic cleansing
And the horror that this brings
I don't pray for missing children
I don't pray for anything
I don't kneel and pray any more
For I can't see the good
I don't believe in God any more
I only wish I could

Rose Horscroft

The Voice Of The Dead

Speaking personally . . .
for the dead . . .
those lost souls,
whose hearts bled.

You wonder why . . .
we went so far,
as to wreck our lives,
it's so bizarre.

You wonder why . . .
we left this coil,
of mortal trouble,
and eternal toil.

We went because . . .
the pain of life,
was more to bear,
than the blade of a knife.

The pills we took . . .
or rope we used,
let our soul free,
from a life, so bruised.

If it was the car we crashed . . .
or lake we used,
to meet our escape . . .
it was not from you!

So rest easy, like we now do . . .
we're sorry for the pain you feel,
. . . forgive us,
we went because . . . we wanted to.

Siobhan O'Conchubhair

Living For Dreams

You'll never make it true.
No matter how hard you try.
I'll never be the same as you.
You can shout and scream.
But I won't play on your team.
I'll only ever play for me.
You can call me strange.
I don't care.
I won't change.
    You told me I couldn't live for dreams.
That I could only ever be a player in your scene.
So I hid.
But now it's time for the come-back kid.
And I'll show you how wrong you were.
I'll show you that I don't have to conform.
And I'll prove
That living for dreams,
Is better than following your rules.

Rachel C Zaino

Villanelle ~ Eastern Europe 1989-99

A chorus of voices will forever shout
against grim tyranny's arrogant fist,
freedom's heart bursts to cry out.

Millions of tongues finally called out
in November's chill and murky mist,
a chorus of voices will forever shout.

Gathering masses caused mounting doubt
for iron systems' withering cyst,
freedom's heart bursts to cry out.

The crowds at the Wall start to rout
the collapsing bricks that cease to exist,
a chorus of voices will forever shout.

Half a million candles parade about,
singing they watch their leaders list,
freedom's heart bursts to cry out.

Reeling under a movement's victory clout
lost leaders rue their chances missed,
a chorus of voices will forever shout,
freedom's heart bursts to cry out.

Robin Perry

Global Warming And Pollution

Once our world was fresh and new,
Covered by forests, fields,
And wild flowers too.
But then, the hand of time,
Spun her web of murk and grime.
Factory chimneys, belched out their smoke,
Turning day into night,
Making everyone choke.
Ever since, the cogs and wheels of time,
Have turned throughout the years,
With coal and gas and oil,
Fought with sweat and tears
And now today, the motorway,
Cars, exhaust fumes, more pollution,
Will we all choke,
Before we find a solution.
Are we too blind to see,
That the power of the sun, the wind and the rain,
Were meant,
To shape our destiny.

Veronica Taylor

How Much Have We Learned?

Each time we fail to see each other as human beings,
We must pray we have not gone irrevocably blind.
Whilst it may be easy enough to be prejudiced,
Is it not easier still to be kind?

God created this world ~ it's not ours.
We are all only here by His grace.
No human being is more precious than another,
In His eyes we *all* have a place.

When Jesus came among us,
He lived among the poor.
So why do we strive to get rich?
Just what do we think we can store?

Money is merely material,
The real treasure lies in the heart.
If I became a millionaire,
Would I truly have more to impart?

Only the most gentle, most humble amongst us,
Actually hear when humanity calls.
By simply crossing the road to their neighbour,
By picking him up when he falls.

By taking a stand for those,
For whom no-one else will stand.
By scaling the walls of ignorance and contempt,
Simply to hold someone's hand.

By reaching out to another human heart,
Even when our own hearts are ailing.
Because none of us are perfect,
Not one of us is without failing.

We all depend upon God's love and His mercy,
And the vast oceans of imperfections it so freely covers.
We know we are totally lost without His compassion,
So why can't we show it to others?

Karen Link

A Song Writer's Dilemma

The hand of controversy
Can snatch away determination
Weakening the foundation of ability
A fair flower grown from seed of deceit
Blowing in the wind of covetousness
Shaking will power vigorously,
Leaving its victim shivering
In the breeze of humility
Clinging to an invisible coat
Lined with instrumental knowledge
Swimming through calm seas of deliverance
Sheltering on white rock of Salvation
Aware of Christ's reflection through skies of blue
Finding reassurance through God's love
Carrying high the flag of faith
Over stones of rapture striking a chord
Releasing a new tune
Captivating melody-winning song is born
Another candle lit
In the world of sacred music.
Dilemma of the song writer's over
Achievement gained through
Mountain of torn pages

Frances Gibson

Silence Please

I simply cannot take it
I absolutely hate it
The blaring 'sound' that is imposed
Upon our suffering ears.

In shops and market places
In restaurants and buses
E'en from our neighbours' houses
And worst of all on beaches . . .

Supposed to be so cheering
It simply leaves me seething
Why do I have to hear
What I don't want to listen to?

Does no one want to think?
Is this the reason for the clamour,
The modern people's banner
Put up to hide behind?

It is impossible to talk
You have to shout above the sound
What is it we're afraid of?
The earth is still going round
And God, its Maker still controls
The sea, the sky, the ground
    We think is ours!

He asks us to be silent
Before His Majesty
So we can hear Him speak
Of joy, of peace, of love,
Throughout eternity.

Olive K Zuurendonk

Forever Yearning

My heart's forever yearning.
As time goes passing by.
I simply can't forget you.
No matter how I try.
You, are always in my dreams at night.
You, are in my thoughts, by day.
No matter just how hard I try.
They just won't go away.
When I look into the mirror.
It's your reflection, there I see.
Maybe those words, you will not speak.
But in your heart, you care.
Maybe we can't relive the past.
Those years, so long ago.
But! We both, have memories.
Of times, we can't let go.
But I will always, love you.
That you surely know.

C W Massey

The Sound Of Silence

The sound of silence
Hits our countryside
Not even a tractor
Just a horrible chill factor
    Utter devastation
    And sheer decimation
Healthy animals their unknown destination,
And farmers, total aggravations.
No lambs gambolling, young calves grazing.
Just fires abalzing.
Folk doing what they could
To try and save their livelihood.
But this disease had taken a hold
There's no hope, so we've been told,
The mass slaughter, of pigs, lambs, and sheep
Whoever's responsible must lose sleep.
But let's hope out of bad comes good,
And our countryside, looks the way it should.

Sheila Buckingham

May Time

The countryside's open again hooray
Well open that is if you're prepared to pay
If you like to see castles and visit gardens so fair
Then jump into your car and take yourself there

Why not oil up your bike and go sightseeing too
Along crowded roads with fume filled queues
With maniac drivers driven to distraction
Taking screaming kids to the latest attraction

What happened to the walking game my favourite thing
The hills stand silent do the birds still sing
The desolate moors bake in the sun
Waiting to welcome us back to the fun

The top boys say it's all over by June
Like the Great War before all done soon
Do they think we were born yesterday
Do they imagine that we've nothing to say

Farmers looking after the country that's a joke
Our heritage is for the common folk
Our right to walk wherever we please
Not a yes you may cross this land by our leave

As an Englishman I have the right
To walk these hills and camp at night
To enjoy the countryside go where I please
Bathe in its rivers shelter under its trees

The palls of smoke the gut churning smell
The bodies of animals too dead to sell
Too dead too really dead to be of any good
Just rotting flesh not suitable for food

We want things back on an even keel
We want to live in a place that's real
Not in a place where life is cheap
And certainly not at the expense of innocent sheep

A Hall

Why Do You Never Listen To Me

How can you be so stubborn in your belief.
How you can profess within my hearing
that our childhood was idyllic
our upbringing achieved with such
care, concern, fairness and felicity

Can you not realise that in the child I was
the silent unyielding secretive child I was,
there hid a person you did not know then
and do not see even now

Did you really not see with what joy I spent
those holidays snatched away from home
Nor the carefree way I tripped off to college
throwing off the shackles of curfews and regulations
Was this not some indication to you
that I had been deeply sorrowful in your house
within that strict regime of selfishness you called
Our family life

Others stormed out, slammed doors,
Wore the clothes their parents hated
Loved the boys they were forbidden

Am I remiss in filial duty, failing to honour as prescribed
Perhaps I fail my grandmother that blessed lady
whom I would protect; honour and love.
For her I tolerate you. Her first child.

Why then do I feel guilty when I find I cannot love you,
Nor even like the person I find you still to be.
Why do I imagine you and I will ever communicate
even as I near fifty and you creak into seventy-one
With arthritis and widowhood your main complaints
How dare I expect that one day you will listen to me

J R Francis

Light

For I should like ~

For I should like
to fill the empty spaces;
the empty spaces
with love and light.

The light of love,
the love of light.

The love of mine
has carried her light
to shine more brightly
in a light more brightly
in a light more brightly lit.

The shadows ebb,
mere wraiths remain.

Footsteps tread
without impression.

The fear of death,
a dread no longer
allaying the fear of living.

Thunder blasts the clouds away,
lightning ignites the vacant spaces.

A voice sings ~
the spaces fill:
'In a light more brightly,
in a light more brightly lit.'

Michael A Fenton

Our World

Our world today is in a terrible state,
Due to men's greed for power, lust and hate,
If only they could be punished and brought to heel,
Made to stand in their victim's shoes, to know how they feel

There are those whose only aim is to push ahead and succeed,
And in doing so, ignoring others and their need,
If only their efforts were channelled into giving aid and relief,
Helping others to happiness instead of perpetual grief

In war stricken countries, how dreadful to see,
Thousands of citizens being made to flee,
From burning homes, with families in retreat,
Struggling to find refuge on aching feet

Helpless we view these scenes, day by day.
Asking why should the innocent have to pay,
Such a high price for freedom, a fair share in life,
Why all the horrors of death, such dreadful strife

If only it were possible to make men understand,
It's not by war, or using a heavy hand.
That problems can be solved to everyone's satisfaction,
But that help and patience should be their course of action

E Kathleen Jones

Remembrance

We gathered round the monument,
The ensigns drooped before.
We listened to the cornet's sound
That echoed from the battle ground.
Our sad thoughts to the men we sent
Away to war.
And in the minutes' silence found
Some comfort in our mutual grief
That young lives shone if all too brief.

Jenny Harrow

Destruction

I hate to see the countryside,
Sprayed with stuff I can't abide,
When I was but a little lass,
'Twas nature study for the class.
We loved the flowers just growing wild,
'Twas pleasure for a little child,
We'd pick some, name them, press in book,
And after years might chance to look.
And find forgotten through the ages,
A dainty flower, within the pages.
Reminding one of days of yore,
Sadly gone, they are no more.

Annie McKimmie

Germm Warfare
(Foot and mouth)

Come with me down on the farm
Let's see what we can see
This is where the cattle fed
And skipped around with glee
This is where the lambs were born
In safety and with care
This is still the farmer
But with glazed and vacant stare

For all his work from year to year
Came to a painful end
Disease was spread across his land
And now his heart must mend

Still silence reigns, the fields are bare
But still the birds do sing
And soon the swallows will arrive
On tired and feathered wing

Farmlife will never be the same
The memories won't die
It's time for deep reflection
And to ask the questions why?

Lin Bourne

Lost

Oaks stand majestic, draped in robes of splendour, green and gold,
Older than time are they, each sown before the written word.
The Saxons, the Jutes, the Danes of old,
Were but acorns when the Picts and Scots fought Arthur's sword.
Where Merlin in his cavern underground,
With dreams and visions of a World in which
The natural ways would all be lost not found,
As Camelot with moat and ditch.

In those times now lost, and gone for good,
When sylphs flew over every beech,
And Juno reigned upon the sylvan wood,
And sprites and nymphs they sought to teach
That every tree a spirit held,
And magical earth stones from celestial places
Stood in circles, men felt compelled
To the sun and stars to turn their faces.

The sowers from the world above,
Provided riches for man's delight.
Both soil and stone he carved with love,
The warmth of Sun, the cool of night.
But people from another land
Usurped the gods of pagan skies,
And armed with bibles did command,
Men turned their backs, and closed their eyes.

Mars and Juno, and other gods by invitations
Sat in judgement of Earth's conduct, broken,
And took from them man's contact with the constellations,
And all pagan gods at last had spoken.
Now the forest keeps its covert council,
And waits in fearful anticipation,
Of man's intent to self destruct,
With greed and mass deforestation.

When, if ever, will mankind comprehend that the damage done will
never mend?
That what is done today at cost, means for us a paradise lost.

Rod Remnant

Remember This

They keep the poor chained with starvation and war,
their children are dying like never before,
falling like corn cut down with a knife,
and those few who live have a pitiful life.

Their government's feasting on all that is best,
look after the few and exploit the rest,
they keep down the masses with the heel of a boot,
and those who stand up in the back they would shoot.

But it's not just the old world, it's happening here,
they're chaining our souls with deception and fear,
they're strangling our schools and health service too,
while lining their pockets they say it's for you.

So we're getting poorer and they're getting rich,
our lives are in ruins, yes! Life is a bitch,
they rob you with taxes the poor pay their due,
with income, VAT, Road and Poll Tax, it all comes from you.

They say that you're lazy and calls us all slobs,
but we don't have a life, if we ain't got no jobs,
so next time you vote the goods there for the taking
let's not regret the chains of our own making.

Jeffrey Kelly

Multi-Coloured Roads

The day of
Multi-coloured roads.
Candy striped telephone poles
And pink elephants,
Will always be,
A vision in my memory,
When war is void,
A world full of joy,
When the global is one,
A world full of peace and unison.

Roisin Drugan

Mankind's Worst Enemy Themselves

The deforestation of the forests
Which has all been caused by man
Is now creating havoc
Across the world's vast span
And is that just not hard lines
How many times before
Have we tried to make contact
With humanity once more
I think they are deaf
I think they are mad
However never mind
Oh and by the way PS I say
I think that they are blind.

Abigail Edna Jones

Peace In The World

To strive for peace
Should be everyone's aim
A mutual feeling to impart
Friendship, loyalty, tolerance
Goodwill and common-sense
Consideration for other people's welfare
The main achievement to gain
A mutual agreement in every heart
Is for love to increase
To war minded citizens stop hell and care
Banish any thought of destruction forever
So let us like a team all endeavour
With one accord attempt to fight
Evil minded people and unite
In keeping a peaceful world
And watch how events are unfurled.

V Stamp

Windblown

Our leaders are terribly clever
They are able to dictate to the breeze,
'Do not spread GM pollen
More than a 300 yard radius please'.

But if there's attack by a virus
It's strange how this very same breeze
Is allowed greater airborne freedom
In fact 3 miles avoids spreading disease!

King Canute tried similar tactics
Telling the sea what he felt it should do,
But it seems the sea wasn't listening ~
Dare the breeze be truculent too?

Irene J Brown

Nuclear War

Button pushed . . .
Mighty red white cloudy explosion.
Mushrooms form continent to continent . . .
1 . . . 2 . . . 3 . . . 4 . . . 5 . . .

Deathly silence . . .
Nothing moving . . .
Black ash soot . . .
Sun erased . . .

Wind begins to blow . . .
Across ruined rubbles plant.
Still, death . . .
Silence . . .

A whisper, a voice heard,
Open door in brilliant sky,
Open arms,
New beginnings.

Derek Robert Hayes

For The Birds

Callaghan's daughter Baroness Jay
Is glad real Lords have had their day.
And Tony's place–men cheer in flocks–
Though 'jay' means 'female chatterbox'.

But 'garrulus glandarius' is a bird,
Also a 'jay', but less absurd.

D P J Smith

Abused

The English are a tolerant race,
Always showing a friendly face,
At least I think we are,
Now alas we are being pushed too far,
We are racist, people accuse,
But who is really guilty of abuse,

We are now a multi-cultural society,
But no one asked us if we wanted to be,
To be English it seems is a sin,
And we have to watch our country go in the bin.
Play the game we beseech,
But they have taken away our right to free speech.

Yet in two world wars people died for this right,
As they all went off to fight,
To make our country a better place,
Lots of people owe their freedom to the English race,
Maybe we should have left them on their own,
And just defended our country alone,
We won the war but lost the peace it's true,
Oh, our wonderful England what will become of you.

Maureen Arnold

Flight Paths

No single cloud despoils the great azure
To hide the silver trails of jets on high
Their flighted paths are safe as they are sure
And there are fifteen thousand reasons why

The tempered altitude is cool and pure
But ancient warnings scream along the sky
As retribution rains down like a cure
The ghosts of futile wars are passing by

What banner can we hoist from flagging mast
What victories are won through hollow fears
By armchair generals lagging in the past
As counterfeit as laptop bombardiers

Reality is virtually extinct
Self virtue now from every pulpit rings
The celluloid records the first to blink
And Hollywood is waiting in the wings

Now play a requiem and let them see
The follies of the centuries complete
Defeat is claimed as moral victory
With victory as hollow as defeat

The hopes of peace are ringing like a bell
But whispered warnings sing out bold alarms
So heed the paradox that leads to hell
Economies depend on, sale of arms!

All hail to these we call our enemy
All hail pariah's nurtured like a rose
We'll raise a glass with all who would be free
But drink the toast to those who may oppose

Barry Morsman

Check-Mate

Twentieth century's world wars
cold wars
fears that Kruschev
or Kosegin, or Yeltsin,
would press the button
bomb the world
whilst drunk, or by mistake,
yet held together just, like a kind of chess
never mind hardly knowing the language

now the USA is developing its anti-missile Bishop
may let the odd one through
yet no protection for the rest of the world

who will send missiles?
Korea, or maybe upstart nations?

Nobody can stop them, new birth or not.

Robert Shooter

A Visit To Parliament

Demonstrators were parading outside the main entrance
The atmosphere was electric and becoming more tense
Placards were being carried with meanings poignant and immense
As they strode up and down there being no pretence

We had passed by The Dome a little earlier that day
And Queen Bodicea's statue just before our short stay
And had spotted the London Eye lifting spectators away
To a very high social level to see London's panoramic display

Our party disembarked after passing Big Ben
In the middle of the protest taking place then
And gathered in a near park to be given the signal when
We could enter the Palace ~ the great British Lion's den

Quietly we filed in to be met by the guard
In the St Stephen's grand entrance where our progress was barred
And waited near two lines of statues on seats which became hard
Before we could proceed when memories somewhere became jarred

We were then shown to a nice tea by our local MP
On the Thames riverside terrace where a great view we did see
And posed for some photographs perhaps two or three
Before exploring the great complex sprouting corridors like a tree

We strolled through Palace Yard after visiting the small shop
Then on to Big Ben where time seemed to stop
And through Westminster Hall and up its wide steps to the top
Before spiralling down to St Stephen's Chapel where Mrs Pankhurst
                                    hid betwixt broom and mop

But the highlight of our tour we still had to come
A short visit to the House of Lords where part of government is run
After penning names and addresses we climbed what seemed a ton
Up flights of narrow steps to see Lords old and young

Then to the House of Commons with procedures just the same
Where climbing to the public gallery now seemed a tiring game
We heard the tellers calling this time a government gain
~ But then we had to go ~ leaving MP's alone again

Keith B Osborne

Life Through My Eyes

To feel one has been neglected
In these times of pollution and strife
Is far short of the truth

We have been neglected by those in power
Mostly because they are too busy
Gathering rose buds whilst they may

Too busy to keep an eye on our cattle and sheep
Wasted meat that could feed thousands
Put clumsily in the earth and fired

We are waiting to vote for one election party
For another four years of hopeful success
Whilst the world is yet more polluted and down trodden

To recently praise that murderer of millions Hitler
The Jews of Germany helped him financially to power
His henchmen obeyed their orders

We can still see happiness abiding
Through a curtain of showery mist
This is very encouraging to the few that know love

To see the first holiday maker
Travelling to the first space hotel on tele
Seems like a mental disarray

We have the wherewithal to bring great joy
Into this wonderful God given world
Stop polluting! Stop hating! Stop thinking of making money!
Just become loving and giving.

Alma Montgomery Frank

Lost

Lost in a field of politics,
With nothing growing but anger.
Where does one go,
When the seeds that we sow,
For our children,
Are lost?
Lost in the promises and maybe's,
Now we're welcoming rabies,
By opening doors,
To the trips and the tours,
From abroad,
What a hoard!
I'm lost!
We're lost in a sea of confusion,
With people full of delusion.
Now ~ Listen ~ they say,
But who are *'they?'*
I'm lost!

Gerry Dymock

I'm British!

I don't want to be part of a super-state,
I'm British, through and through!
I don't want some bureaucrat in Brussels
Telling me what to do!

I swear allegiance to a sovereign,
Not a self-made politician.
Stability grown through the centuries,
Not a whim, or ill-thought decision.

I don't want to lose my identity
To some foreign potentates,
I want what's best for my country,
Not a speck in a potage of states.

I think of the millions who've given their lives
That we might have freedom of choice,
To live in this green and pleasant land,
With the privilege to speak as one voice.

Our history is not all rich and glorious,
For we have made mistakes,
But that's how we've grown to become what we are ~
Great Britain, not a European state!

Joan Thompson

We Fought Fascism

We fought fascism
For the material and the money men
We fought fascism
For the billion dollar organisation
And we fought fascism
For sexual awareness in the middle classes
And we fought fascism
For the porno stars and the lap dancers
We fought them for the stock exchange
Viagra pills, Burger King
Cheap thrills, sure
We fought fascism
And won too much of everything
And we forgot
And we learnt nothing

Rhod Bevan

Just Another Day
(Written after the 'Omagh' bombing)

People rushing all around,
Busy shopping, merry sound,
Children whining, not much fun,
Bright blue sky, shining sun,
Traffic speeding, must watch out,
Parked cars, they're safe no doubt.

The only danger here is man,
But no one knows his devious plan,
How they can look on this happy place
With no remorse is a big disgrace,
But they shall reap their just reward,
On the day that they meet the Lord.

So, innocently they go their way,
Something forgotten, well there's another day,
Perusing merrily, around a shop,
Something makes this family scene stop,
A gigantic explosion rips the air,
These so called men hide in their lair.

People laying all around,
Screaming crying, is the sound,
Children whimpering, that's no fun,
Blackened sky, with no sun,
Traffic still, must watch out
For parked cars, not safe no doubt.

Marie Mullings

The Life-Saving Ozone

God made the earth in six short days,
And found it was good, so the Bible says.
He set it spinning on its endless flight
Round the sun which He gave for warmth and light.

And the earth was a most wonderful creation,
From its highest pinnacle to its deepest ocean.
He filled it with life of every kind;
Plants, fish, birds, animals and mankind.

And the sun shone down to nourish them all,
That constant, ever-friendly fiery ball
As it's done while millions of years have gone by;
To God they are but the twinkling of an eye!

But now it would seem we have displeased God,
And the bounds of decency have been over-trod,
For in our folly we are destroying the air,
And the sun's rays no longer have the same care.

They beat down, unfiltered, and cause disease,
While man sits, unheeding, apparently at ease.
This situation cannot be allowed to go on;
We must do all we can to restore the ozone.

Marlene Allen

Unsaintly Poet

Like silken sounds the songs he spun,
He seemed to have listened-in on high
And heard the seraphim sing ~
Even mundane minds he raised to the sky.

In the Library, a rare, cherished book he'd borrow
Always just before I came: I forgave
His tardiness, hoping that one good morrow
He'd be finished with it; and on I pored over Palgrave.
One Monday, another sat in his accustomed nook,
I never saw him again, *nor* that much coveted book.

Mary Frances Mooney

Lost

The children play in the dip
        between the hills
Their voices carry on the wind
        you hear their shrills
Then as you look you see them climb
        climb up and over
Until they disappear from view
        midst their dreams of clover
They are swept into the sky
        hand in hand
Floating out of reach
        way above the land

There you gaze once more
        between those hills
Old men and women singing
        you hear their trills
Then as you look you see them change
        change from old to young
Until they interchange.
        ~ Their lamenting song is sung
They lament for their youth
        the youth they lost
Fighting in the fields of glory
        the world does count the cost!

   G Carpenter

I'm English

English I was born and English I shall die.
No power in Europe can take this precious gift from me:
No political clap-trap can stop my wayward thoughts.
　　English born and bred: I am free!

British I accept, though what does that mean today?
I love my neighbours, Welsh and Scots and Celts across the sea.
No one can tell me whom to hate and whom to love.
　　I'm English: I am free!

For centuries this island has given hope to those in need,
From Africa and India and other lands across the sea.
We've welcomed them, their skills, their special ways,
　　And now, in England, they are free.

So Downing Street and Whitehall, just stop your silly ways,
Telling us what we may do and even think and say.
It really doesn't work, all this so-called PC.
Don't you know that we don't listen?
　　We are free!

Martha Fear

April Stroll

There's a little known, seldom articulated,
scientific principle, according to which,
Safeways trolleys, like iron filings
to a magnet, are
irresistibly attracted
to canals.

Humanity (God's handiwork!) is an obscenity
on the fair face of nature, forever besmirching
its actual or potential loveliness, forever fouling
its own nest, like a seagull or an albatross
with diarrhoea, permanent fits
of the runs.

Mile after mile of plastic-covered reeds,
junk crucified on trees, condoms
from the condominium, assorted bottles, tins,
unspeakable lengths of this and that,
a splendid pram, apparently untenanted,
several blood-red rubber gloves,
spookily fingerless.

Why do we do it?
Why such disrespect?
So much irreverence?

Amid the squalor and the sad detritus, nature
resurgent and redemptive. A white-collared mallard
on a garden wall, head-feathers bottle-green, a Castrol-
coloured sheen. Two busy coot construction-workers.
Fugitives from captivity, great sun-bursts of wild daffodils.

The swans this year have moved 500 yards: the dance
of the little cygnets a quarter of a mile
nearer, my God, to Glasgow.

Norman Bissett

Unfair System

I am not in love with Capitalism
    as it is a system so unfair
It caters to the moneyed class
    and for its poor it doesn't care

There are those who are rich and wealthy
    whose lives are all secure
Whilst neighbours living next to them
    are struggling because they're poor

I think Politics here are needing changed
    to create a Just Society
And never to have differences
    where the wealthy have propriety

Those who have money to excess
    should help the poor folk out
And if this system was in vogue
    then maybe none would be without

There are some where money is their God
    who wouldn't like this changed
But I can see some troublesome times
    if a fairer system is not arranged

Lachlan Taylor

The Colossus Of Gateshead

Eight hundred, thousand pounds, now what could it buy?
With such a sum, priorities would vie.
Re-open hospital wards ~ a worthwhile goal,
Employ a hundred teachers still on the dole.
Buy books and equipment, saving the PTAs,
Repair roads and buildings well into decay.
No! A brilliant idea ~ erect a monstrosity,
The Colossus of Gateshead ~ arouse curiosity!
A big, brash, banal, sexless figure,
Feet set in concrete, wings couldn't be bigger!
Angel of the North, the name given to it,
But the religious connotation does not fit.
Biblical angels are comforting and warm,
Appearing to reassure freedom from harm.
This looming from the mist suddenly on the A1
Could frighten the life out of anyone.
This blatantly, ugly steel fabrication
Embodies the twisted values of this nation.
Millions poured each week into the lottery draw,
More money to play with than ever before.
Man's ideas have run wild, imagination soared,
This time the forgotten North East has scored.
So, the Angel of the North spreads its rusty wings,
But, devoid of meaning, no solace it brings!

Pat Heppel

Litter

Flicking it here, flicking it there,
Litter louts are everywhere!

Packets from crisps or toothsome sweets
Abound in hundreds on our streets.
Tickets from buses, coach or train
Accumulate and block each drain.

Flicking it here, flicking it there,
Litter louts are everywhere!

Under the hedges bottles hide
And tin cans lurk both far and wide.
Wrappings from chips and fish as well
Thrown down to make the litter swell.

Flicking it here, flicking it there,
Litter louts are everywhere!

And yet the litter bins abound,
On every street they can be found,
So why, oh why, is there no place
Where beauty they do not deface?

Flicking it here, flicking it there,
Litter louts are everywhere!

Roma Davies

The Golden Words

The golden words I love you
Will never never be heard
By my earthlings ears
The warm and tender touch
Of your angels soft hands
Will never never be felt
By my earthlings body
And the fast beat of your angels heart Marie
Will never be felt in reality
By my earthlings heart ever

Because you Marie are an angel
A very beautiful angel
From high up in heaven above
An angel of beauty who has never
Come down to earth at all

So the one and only time
My sweet loving angel Angila Marie
I will ever hear those words I love you
Feel the touch of your tender hands
Or feel the beat of your angel's tender heart
Next to mine at anytime
Is in my heavenly dreams at night

Donald Tye

Foot And Mouth Disease

Come on Salley I say to my dog
Instead of a walk let's go for a jog
Little does Salley know what is in store
No frolicking in field and wood
No ball games
What a restricted walk along the lanes
Cars are passing to and fro
Is it to business or pleasure they go?
Poor Salley cannot understand what's spoilt her world
Oh that the mystery would unfurl
One day healthy lambs frisk and play
The next they are put in lorries to be taken away. And destroyed
Because of the foot and mouth disease
Poor farmers how they must feel ill at ease
The cattle who have contracted this disease
Must be slaughtered as well
So much the Government do in immunisation for people
Why can't we care for animals too
They have a place on Earth for me and you
Why are the Government so mean with their money
Surely that's something that is not funny
Farmers be not too dismayed
The answer will come to help you continue your trade.

Y Rossiter

Land Of Soap And Tory
(With apologies to Land of Hope and Glory)

Land of soap and Tory, never we'll be free.
Both will have us brainwashed, as long as we've TV.
Just because we're 'Neighbours', does that make us 'Friends'?
Living in the 'Street' where we've Tories at both ends!

They tell us that life's better, when the Tories make the rules,
They must think that we're crazy, a lot of stupid fools.
No wonder we're so hard up and resort to moneylenders,
It's enough to drive us to 'Old Vic' and booze with the 'Eastenders'!

It's just as bad in Yorkshire where Jack Sugden farms the land,
In 'Emmerdale', that farm where things get really out of hand.
Of course, he blames the Tories for his constant lack of cash,
It could, of course, be 'Brookside' that makes the programmes clash!

We arrive at last at life's 'Crossroads' to be halted by 'The Bill',
Who advise us to go 'Home and Away', let the Tories have their fill.
The plots and plans in all these soaps will make your 'Heartbeat'
faster,
But knowing they'll be there next week will avert complete disaster!

Of course, there are the *real* soaps, whose ads are always right,
'Hold this in your 'Palm-Olive' out in the bright 'Sunlight'.'
But with those gorgeous creamy 'Lux' that gets me in a lather,
She says, 'Not on your 'Lifebuoy', that's how I met your Father!'

G K (Bill) Baker

Save Your Vote

With a lump in my throat
I tell the people save your vote.
No Prime Minister will ever care
How can you vote for Tony Blair.
We know Tory policies are too vague
So you can't vote for William Hague.
Like so many I have seen
From Lib-Dem or the Green.

Widdicombe and Short are tarty
Don't ever vote for either party.
Most ministers talk a lot
Just take a look at John Prescott.
Tony Blair is just a clown
With his mate that Gordon Brown.
What is the election really for
To elect a fool like that Jack Straw.

Give this advice to your neighbour
No Lib-Dem Tory or silly Labour.
Who would you like to be the boss
On the paper don't put your cross.
There is just one thing to say
Stay in on Election Day.
On that paper won't see my name
For all those parties are all the same.

Colin Allsop

Life Today

As I walk along the street
I study the faces of people I meet
Their worried looks no hint of a smile
Wondering if life is really worthwhile
Jobs and Hospitals closing down
All over the country in every town
The old the sick are being forgotten
People from all walks of life at rock bottom
Food prices and charges all still rise
The government don't heed the people's cries
They sit in parliament and dish out rules
Don't worry about our Kids or our schools
Those in Power won't give way or bend
Oblivious of lives that once shattered won't mend
Their lives are different from the ordinary man
They will take all we give But give the least they can.

E M Catlin

The Secret Speech

Too oft' in past civilisations the speech
Of many silenced where it was preached
The voice of those could speak or even teach
And writings observed each to each.
Bold proclamation not known now, unreachable
As high observance in past fable tabled
In secrecy and other treachery without label
On freedom's threshold, no rule for the stable.

In lands too where democracy was not born
Nor wise declaim from church to be born
The demigod or dictator professed a creed torn
With great care where it should be foresworn.
To what is writ and can be told
From the empower'd in much sought gold
From new embattlements warring new or old
For those in wanton words and act too bold.

If the book could yet be opened
And every message all could send
Our real wishes or country to defend
It is not penned
Now science plays an ill-met part
Dark secrets speak but do not impart
Their dreaded vision in torture, unnatural dangers in much
                                        devious art
In too much death nor no new high enterprise to start.

Speeches still delivered on such freedom
For the many, new times made real for any for man and animals, oft'
                                        not seldom.

John Amsden

Zero Tolerance

On Sunday, which was the thirteenth,
Though that is neither here nor there,
I found that some person or persons unknown
Had tried to enter my home ~
Uninvited.
He, for however politically incorrect it may be
That is how I think of this person,
Had attacked my window with a screwdriver,
Wrecking the locking mechanism,
Failing to open it,
Achieving nothing.
Except that the window must be replaced
For now it will not open,
While remaining not quite shut.

Probably this person comes from a broken home,
Is terrorised by police brutality
And takes drugs in some form
To blot out the reality of his sad life.
Kindly magistrates would express sympathy
And allot him a personal counsellor
Who would arrange a nice holiday for him ~
Not that he ever works
So strictly does not need one.

But me, if I could get my hands on him,
I'd break his legs.

Ann Harrison

Junk Mail

I only have a pension small,
For bills and food I need it all,
Yet ev'ry day inside my door
The letters lie there wanting more.

I know that children have a need,
That animals, like us, must feed,
That many people have no home
And through the streets are forced to roam.

Disaster strikes in foreign land
And Oxfam write with begging hand;
From my small mite I send ten pounds
And this then draws the hunting hounds.

Although I tell them I am poor
Yet still they ask for more and more.
I wish they'd understand and switch
Their supplications to the rich.

If politicians got this mail,
Or wealthy bankers, would they fail
To ease the suff'ring that we see,
Could they not do much more than me?

And if these rich folk do not give
To help the needy ones to live
Surely to beg from such as me
Will never solve the misery.

So all you groups with good intent
Please let us old folk live content;
Don't make our thoughts seem guilty, please
Let us live our lives in peace.

The Wandering Bard

God's Universe
*(Ps.146 'Do not put your trust in princes, in mortal men,
who cannot save')*

Jesus, You and Your Father
By the Spirit, lovingly created our world:
Create all, still.
Now men, Your creation, interfere with its laws.

God is omnipresent
He is biding His time.
Our Lady interceding with Him,
For mercy for us, who offend Him.

You children of God
Who abuse the Father's Laws
Interfere with Genetics
Interfere with the seed of crops for gain,
So that nations go hungry . . .

. . . He sees what you do
And there will be a Reckoning.
This life is but a brief span.
Do not kill His children!
You, who are the real stewards of His Kingdom today.

H Smith

Teachers

Traumatised, like standing stones,
Tormented by wind,
Battered by rain,
We stood a long time braving the elements
Until, finally, one by one,
We fell sideways,
Headlong into the long grass,
The fuchsia'd hedgerows, foxgloved bogs
And crevices of burned abbeys and broken graves.
Still we fell,
Like loose change, jingling from a torn pocket,
Scattered coins
Rolling on to a vast beach,
To settle in the sunlight:
Content to listen to the waves;
Each in our own solitude,
Hidden in the sand.

Penelope Freeston

Sweet 'n' Sour

The lamb is a symbol for Christians,
They link it with God's name,
But they kill them whilst they are babies
And eat them, just the same.

We all love chicks at Easter,
Small, yellow and fluffy of course.
Then we cut their throats and bleed them
To serve with white wine sauce.

Pheasants in full plumage
Make a bright blaze in the sky,
But they're not bred for their beauty,
They're just born to die.

And rabbits are sweet on the hillside,
Unlike the fox, who is cruel.
So we gave them myxomatosis.
Who are we trying to fool?

So don't get friendly with humans
If you're cuddly and cute.
They'll say, 'Oo' and 'Ah', very friendly,
Then use you to eat or shoot.

E A Kibbler

Freedom Of Speech

'Do we guard our freedom of speech we hold so dear?
Oft a word so critical and indiscreet we make without fear.
We have no compunction to criticise those that lead
We even comment that why do we have them, is there a need?
On sad reflection our modern world still has its dictators
Some systems are set-up harsh and brutal by its creators.
We look at each continent and learn of the oppressed
If one has a liberal mind it's difficult to digest.
Our world we take for granted and in our stride
We are free and do not have the need to hide.
But, we must with caution jealously guard this right,
And, resist having freedom of speech stolen without a fight.
So let us now reflect, look forward and rejoice
And maintain this freedom with a unified voice.'

Peter E Parbery

Ode To Human Frailty

How can we presume to feel
So personally betrayed
When, sadly, the highly revered
Often fall from grace . . .
Victims of their own human failings?

For, isn't it true, that perfection
Is something only eluded to
But, never truly achieved?

Isn't it something, we, ourselves
Have tried to capture . . .
Only to realize we're unable
To quite manage somehow?

Why do we expect perfection
From our heroes,
When we're unable to achieve it . . .
For ourselves?

Perfection . . .
Oh, how we all strive for it!
How we all aspire to it!
But, alas, in the end . . .
Discover . . . we're merely human, after all!

Mary Beth Bott

A Matter Of Ethics

Nothing brings out more ambition
Than the challenge of direct competition
In politics, the work force, sports, in every day situations,
Unfortunately, it can sometimes strain friendly relations,
Competing for power or promotion in any profession
Creating attitudes of superiority or aggression
And perceptions of being indispensable
Initiating circumstances reprehensible
While stepping on toes to reach goals
That infringe on time and talent.
Better not to damage reputation of others, such foils
But to portray character that is gallant,
To curb over-zealous inclinations
To be principled in aspirations
Leading to prosperity and good fortune,
Paving the way to a commensurate portion
Of happiness along with wealth,
Of accomplishment, serenity and good health.

Flossie

Too Late

The jogger ran by the old homestead;
On its large, overgrown yard
Were kids running in the sprinkler.
She waved and thought someday
 ~ someday she'd stop by
    and bring her kids
The golfer drove by the homestead;
On its wrapped-around porch and in its swing
Were families breaking bread.
He waved and thought someday
~ someday he'd stop for awhile
    and bring the juice to drink.
The executive rushed by the quiet homestead;
At its opened, double doors
Stood couples, she and he, he and he, and she and she.
But he was juggling phone and wheel
~ and didn't think to stop
    and come in.
The tired mom dreamed of the rambling homestead;
Inside its high arched windows
Could be seen folks standing and chatting.
She watched it from across a street
~ and then awoke confused:
    where was she?
Then the jogger, the golfer, the executive, and the tired mom
came by the old homestead and its overgrown lawn,
    it's porch and swing, its double door, and its arched windows,
but the lawn was empty, and the swing was still,
    the doors were closed, and the windows shuttered.
One by one, they walked away . . .

John A Mills